Bianconi & Butler of Tipperary

By Art Kavanagh

License Notes

This ebook is licensed for your personal enjoyment only. This ebook may not be re-sold or given away to other people. If you would like to share this book with another person, please purchase an additional copy for each recipient. If you're reading this book and did not purchase it, or it was not purchased for your use only, then please return to createspace.com and purchase your own copy. Thank you for respecting the hard work of this author.

Bianconi & Butler of Tipperary

Copyright © Art Kavanagh 2013

First published 2013

All rights reserved. Without limiting the rights under copyright reserved above, no part of this publication may be reproduced, stored in or introduced into a database and retrieval system or transmitted in any form or any means (electronic, mechanical, photocopying, recording or otherwise) without the prior written permission of both the owner of copyright and the above publishers.

Original illustrations/ Photographs

Bianconi & Butler of Tipperary

Kavanagh, Art

Table of Contents

Bianconi & The Corpse Under The Bed 1

Bianconi's Humble Beginnings 2

Bianconi Moves To Clonmel 3

Bianconi Starts His Public Transport Business 4

Bianconi Marries Eliza Hayes 6

Bianconi Becomes A Naturalized Citizen 7

Bianconi Becomes Mayor of Clonmel & Buys Longfield 10

Tragedy Strikes the Bianconi Family 13

Lord Cahir's Siblings Kidnapped 15

The Origin of the Butlers of Cahir 16

The Butlers of Cahir in the $17^{th}/18^{th}$ Centuries 19

Richard the 10th Lord Cahir 22

Law & Order on the Butler Estates 23

Richard Butler the Last Lord Cahir 24

Bianconi

Bianconi & The Corpse Under The Bed

The Chief Secretary of Ireland once asked Bianconi how, he, a foreigner, had acquired such a distinguished position in Ireland. Bianconi had replied: "Well, it was because, while the big and the little were fighting, I crept up between them, carried out my enterprise and obliged everybody."

There is a good story told about Bianconi and his trusted agent Dan Hearn. In the mid 1830s, Bianconi, accompanied by Dan Hearn was out driving around the country inspecting cars and visiting agents. Occasionally they would have to spend the night away from home. One night coming from Thurles they had to take lodgings at a carman's stage, which was managed by a woman called Biddy Minehan. Biddy had only one room vacant and the two men had to share the bed. Neither could sleep. Dan, who was feeling cold, put his hand under the bed saying, "There must be an iceberg under here". With that he jumped out of the bed and raced down the stairs to the kitchen where the carmen were smoking and drinking. He then shouted up the stairs "come down, Mr.B., come down out of that". Bianconi immediately jumped out of the bed and went down to see what the commotion was.

"Did you see it?" asked Dan.
"See what?"
"The Devil" whispered Dan, shaking with fright.
"Where?" queried Bianconi.
"Under the bed," was the frightened reply. Biddy Minehan came forward.
"I had no place else to put it your Honour."
"Put what?" enquired Bianconi.
"The corpse, your Honour," she replied, "we were going to have a wake when you came asking for lodgings, and I thought it would be hard to lose the chance of a few shillings, so having no bed to spare I just slipped the corpse under the bed"

One day, while being driven in a carriage in London, Bianconi noticed a rather stout man trying in vain to hire a carriage. He ordered his driver to pull over and invited the man to travel with him. The grateful stranger got in and enquired the name of his generous host. Bianconi told him his name.
"The great Bianconi!" he exclaimed. Bianconi then, politely, asked his passenger what his name was.
"Rothschild", was the reply. Bianconi regretted all his life that he hadn't the presence of mind to say "The great Rothschild!"

Bianconi's Humble Beginnings

This extraordinary man, a penniless immigrant Italian, became a very wealthy man who made the transition to become one of the gentry of Tipperary in a seamless and effortless manner.

While this had been done before by numerous families including the Bagwells and Grubbs of Clonmel, it had taken at least a couple of generations to achieve what Bianconi did in his own lifetime.

He arrived in Ireland in 1802 at the age of sixteen. He was brought over from Italy by Andrea Faroni, a man who made prints of famous pictures. Faroni brought three other young apprentices with him. Originally he had intended to go to London, but for some strange reason he chose to go to Dublin instead. Upon arrival he collected any money the apprentices had and used it to set up his business. Bianconi had a hundred gold coins, which had been given to him by his family and friends and this was reluctantly handed over.

Faroni set up shop in Dublin and began to manufacture prints. He sent young Charles Bianconi out into the streets of Dublin to sell the prints. The young lad knew no English except what he had been told to say "buy, buy, buy".

Within a short time, when his command of the language improved, his master sent him out to the countryside towns to sell his wares. He travelled to most of the counties and towns in Leinster and to Waterford and Tipperary in Munster. His master supplied him with two pounds worth of pictures and four pence subsistence money.

Later one of the other apprentices was sent with Bianconi but he became restless and ran away. Another boy, Ribaldi,[1] was sent in his place and they continued selling their wares in the country towns.

One day, in Passage, in Waterford, Bianconi was arrested for selling a picture of Napoleon, although the Peace of Amiens had been declared the previous year. He was suspected of being a French agent. Fortunately for him the magistrate decided to release him without charge.

When his apprenticeship was over in 1804 Faroni gave his apprentices their money, which he had held in trust. Bianconi immediately began to invest his money in buying prints and in making a box with shoulder straps to carry them. After some months of trudging the roads with the very weighty pack he decided to settle down for a few months and did so in Thurles. There he met a young man who was to become his life-long friend. He was Toby Mathew, later to become Fr. Theobald Mathew, the apostle of Temperance.

He didn't stay very long in Thurles and soon moved on to Cahir, where he stayed a while with a family named Baldwin. From there he went to Carrick-on-Suir where he opened his first shop. Because he needed to go to Waterford for his supplies he found the journey by boat intolerable. It only went once a week and on one occasion he was soaked with the rain, as a result of which he developed pleurisy. When he had recovered he decided to move to Waterford. He got an introduction to Edmund Rice, the founder of the Christian Brothers, who took it upon himself to continue Bianconi's education.

Bianconi Moves To Clonmel

After two years in Waterford he made up his mind to move to Clonmel. At that time, in 1809, Clonmel was a prosperous trading

---

[1] Ribaldi eventually became a retailer of mirrors and set up shop in Limerick and later moved to London. The fourth lad, Castelli, opened a picture shop in Waterford and became quite prosperous.

town of some 18,000 inhabitants. There were breweries, distilleries and factories producing cotton and linen goods.

He opened a shop in a good location and began trading. His landlord was Bagwell of Marlfield. Bianconi was a good listener and became interested in the local politics. He became friendly with the Grubbs and other Quakers.

His business thrived and he was very fortunate in getting a contract to buy up all the golden guineas hoarded by the peasantry. He made substantial profits from this venture and he continued to expand and reinvest in his business.

Charles Bianconi now found that he had to travel to Dublin occasionally on business. There he met and became friendly with the Patron of the Italians residing in Ireland. The Patron, Signor Del Vecchio, lived near the sea in a house rented from a Mr. Philpot Hayes, a wealthy stockbroker, who also lived close by. Bianconi became quite friendly with the Hayes family and there he met the five-year-old Eliza Hayes who was to become his wife.

It was at the Hayes household that Bianconi met Daniel O'Connell for the first time. O'Connell said of this meeting later that he found a young man 'looking up at me with a face seen only on a Roman coin'.

Down in Clonmel Bianconi was making his presence felt too. The public library was a place where Catholics were expected to talk in whispers while the Protestant had the right to express their views in louder tones. One day Bianconi began an animated discussion in a loud voice and was joined by others. From then on Catholic and Protestant stated their views on equal terms.

Bianconi Starts His Public Transport Business

The next big milestone in Bianconi's career was his idea of starting a public transport business. It was 1814 and the war in Europe was over. Grain prices had fallen from an astronomical 3s.8d. per stone to 1s.per stone. Army horses were plentiful and cheap. As there was a tax on private vehicles many of them were laying idle.

Bianconi

In June of the following year his first coach set out from Clonmel to Cahir carrying the mail for Cahir post office at half the fee normally paid by the Government. Passengers were slow to avail of the service and Bianconi had to resort to a ruse to promote interest in the venture. He bought and outfitted another car without letting anyone know he was the owner. The two cars began racing each other. Bets were made as to which car would arrive first. Soon people began travelling in both cars to enjoy the race at first hand.

He now extended the range and routes of the cars and went west as far as Limerick and north to Thurles and Cashel. Soon after he initiated a service to Waterford.

Staff had to be employed and complex organizational ability was needed. Bianconi was up to the task and soon his cars became known the length and breath of the land. They were called Bians for short and on occasion the man himself was called Bian, which he took as a compliment.

In a remarkable incident in his life in 1826 Bianconi became embroiled in the bitterness of Irish politics. Lord George Beresford, the brother of the Marquess of Waterford, stood for election in that

Arriving at the end of a stage

year. He hired Bianconi coaches to bring his voters to the polls. As there was no liberal candidate Bianconi agreed to have his coaches used for this purpose. At the last minute Mr. Villiers Stuart came forward to oppose Lord George and support Catholic Emancipation. O'Connell supported Mr. Stuart. In those days it took three days to complete the polls. On the first day the Bians carrying the Beresford voters were attacked and heaved over the bridge. Bianconi himself, though a firm supporter of the liberals and a member of the Catholic Association, was pelted with mud.[2] He immediately contacted the Beresford agent and terminated the agreement as he could not, he said 'risk property and the lives of his drivers'. The agent concurred. Bianconi then put his coaches at the disposal of Villiers Stuart who won the election comfortably.

Bianconi Marries Eliza Hayes

The following year, when Bianconi was forty years old, he married Eliza Hayes. In the marriage settlement made with her father Bianconi settled £2000 on his wife and children, while Mr. Hayes settled £1200 on his daughter. They were married in Dublin, in the Hayes house, by Archbishop Murray, a family friend.

After the wedding they went to Clonmel where they were met by a huge crowd of well-wishers. In time-honoured fashion the horses were unharnessed and the coach was drawn through the streets of Clonmel by the cheering workmen. From the balcony in their apartment the bride and groom looked out and were cheered even more loudly. Then the fiddles started up and the Bians (coachmen and workers) sang a song specially composed for the occasion called "The Coachman's Song".

'Now welcome lovely lady,
To this country by the Suir,
Where yer fine man started going
The Bians that will endure.

---

[2] He was also a member of the Order of Liberators, a society formed by O'Connell with a view to conciliate Irishmen of all classes and creeds, prevent feuds and faction fights and to discourage secret societies. As the head of the Order, O'Connell was accorded the title of 'The Liberator'.

'Tis we are proud to greet ye
And we hope ye are the same,
For before the God Almighty
Ye're a great and lovely Dame.

And to ye, yer honour, Sir,
We sing our song as well,
To wish ye years of plenty
In this grand and lovely dell;
To tell ye that we'll always
Take our horses to the end,
And may ye meet but happy days
Round every single bend.'

In the next year, 1828, Bianconi's daughter, Catherine, was born and Daniel O'Connell was elected an M.P. for Clare. As in the election of Villiers Stuart the Bianconi cars brought the Clare voters to the polls. Within a year the Catholic Emancipation Bill was passed.

Bianconi Becomes A Naturalized Citizen

Bianconi, a Catholic, was still considered an alien, as Daniel O'Connell pointed out to him at a dinner in Merrion Square. As such he could not purchase land in Ireland. O'Connell offered to approach Sir Robert Peel the Prime Minister with a view to introducing a Private Bill to have Bianconi naturalized. As this procedure would be very costly he suggested an alternative. Bianconi drew up a memorial for the Viceroy showing how he had come to Ireland and the path his career took since then. He was directed to obtain testimonials from the principal magistrates in the district and a certificate from at least one member of the Privy Council. He was naturalized in 1831 by Royal decree.

In 1833 he went to London to seek contracts from the Government for the conveyance of cross mails. He had contacts in the Whig government and was able to get an interview with the Postmaster General, the Duke of Richmond. He took an instant liking to Bianconi and when Bianconi returned to Ireland he had the contract for the mails.

Dropping a Passenger

Shortly after this he was notified of his father's death and discovered that he had been left a quarter of his land holdings in Italy. Bianconi travelled back to Italy taking only one servant. He stayed with his family there for a couple of weeks and made over the property to his nephew. He paid substantial sums to save his nephews having to join the army and set up a fund for their education.

Back in Ireland he moved house to get his complaining household away from the stables and coach yards. He bought a property, which became known as Spring House. Many famous people came to dine there including the Liberator, Lord Monteagle, and most of the Tipperary M.P.s such as Thomas Wyse, Richard Lalor Shiel, Mr. Justice Ball and Lewis Perrin who became Chief Baron Wolfe. Other members of the O'Connell clan came to visit too, brothers[3] and nephews of the Liberator, who himself often stayed there days at a time.

---

[3] One of these was John of Grena, a huge man who bore on his face the scar of a bullet wound received in one of his eighteen duels.

Bianconi

In 1835 Daniel O'Connell formed the National Bank of Ireland and became its first Governor. It was intended to help the poorer people to avail of banking facilities. The Clonmel National Bank was opened in the same year and Bianconi became one of its directors and principal shareholders.

Sometime shortly after this O'Connell was found to be in financial difficulty himself and it was Bianconi with two other friends who sorted out his affairs.

Bianconi at the time of his marriage

Despite his generosity in some ways he could be mean. There is a story that he brought back a tea urn from London and brought it to Hearn's hotel where he gave it to Judy, the barmaid. A day or two later he called and told Judy she owed him 5s 9d. She enquired what that was for. "For the tea urn", he replied. Judy was flabbergasted and said she thought it was a present.

"Not at all," said Bianconi, "come pay me what you owe me". She gave him 5s 8d. which was all the money in the till. The next day he came back looking for the balance of 1d.

Bianconi did not see eye to eye with O'Connell on the Repeal of the Union. He felt that rule from Westminster was fair and impartial especially under a liberal government. Nevertheless his personal loyalty to the Liberator was such that he never openly criticized his policies.

Bianconi Becomes Mayor of Clonmel & Buys Longfield

He was elected Mayor of Clonmel in 1844 and had to buy his own robes of office and chain as the other robes and chain had been removed by the Tory corporation, along with all the legal books of reference. He also provided a stand for the Corporation regalia, which consisted of a sword with a Toledo blade and two silver maces dating from the reign of Charles II. He wrote to O'Connell to ask him how to discharge his civic duties and what legal books he should consult. O'Connell replied as follows – ' if you wish to discharge the duties of mayoralty with perfect satisfaction, act upon your own sound common sense and do not look into any law books'.

He was the first Catholic Mayor of Clonmel to wear his mayoral robes to Mass. It was pointed out to him that this was in contravention of the law but Bianconi persisted and the matter was overlooked by the authorities.

As Mayor he was also a Justice of the Peace and as such presided over the Borough Petty Sessions, assisted by two Resident Magistrates. He was reputed to be just but firm in his dealings with the petty offenders who came before him. He was very generous to the poor and needy and gave considerable sums to have National Schools built in the town.

In 1846 the Longfield estate, which Bianconi had admired from his youth, came on the market. The owner, Captain Edward Long had become depressed after the murder of his father. This combined with the reduced rents due to the famine made him decide to leave Ireland. Bianconi paid £22,000 for the beautiful house and estate.

Longfield (courtesy Irish Architectural Archive)

When he moved to Longfield with his family he was met by the Cashel Temperance Band and cheering crowds of employees, tenants and servants. This was extraordinary in the time of the famine. A great party was held on the lawn with singing and dancing and refreshments. An address of welcome was read and in reply Bianconi emphasized the need for everyone to do their duty properly, landlord and tenant, mechanic and labourer. He exhorted everyone to obey the law and to be temperate as recommended by his good friend Fr. Mathew and by the Liberator.

One of the first things Bianconi did was to send to Italy for experts to lay out an Italian garden. He also planted a rose garden with white and yellow roses to represent the Joyful Mysteries of the Rosary and red roses for the Sorrowful Mysteries.

Here he entertained the Grubbs, the Maudes of Dundrum and the Coopers of Killenure, while he in turn was entertained in other Big Houses. He was particularly pleased to have been invited to the Viceregal Lodge where he was entertained by the Viceroy, the Earl of Bessborough.

During the worst years of the famine he was in a position to alleviate the rents of the tenants and provide works, such as building a demesne wall, to enable the poor to earn money. He also set up a soup kitchen and provided meals of macaroni and got a Frenchman, who lived in Cashel to give lessons to the people on how to cook the Italian food.

Because his eldest daughter Catherine developed tuberculosis in 1850, Bianconi was advised that she should spend time in a warm climate so he decided to bring his family to the Italy. This time he travelled in style bringing three coaches, his own horses and a large number of servants. He was to spend three years in Italy while his daughter languished in her illness. The family was given an audience with the Pope and Bianconi's son, Charles, was made a papal Chamberlain. This was a signal honour and it entailed young Charles having to attend the Papal Court at certain times of the year dressed in an exotic medieval type of dress.

Daniel O'Connell had died in 1847 and in accordance with his wishes his heart was buried in Rome. Bianconi commissioned a monument, which was erected in the Church of St. Agatha, which is in the Irish College in Rome, to remember his great friend. This is the inscription which he had written on the monument:

This Monument contains the Heart of
O'CONNELL
Who, dying on the way to the Eternal City, bequeathed

> His Soul to God, his Body to Ireland,
> And his Heart to Rome.
> He is represented at the Bar of the British House of Commons
> 1829
> when he refused to take the anti-Catholic declaration
> in these remarkable words;
> "I at once reject this declaration: part of it I believe to be untrue,
> and the rest I know to be false."
> He was born on 6th August 1776; died 15th May 1847.
> Erected by Charles Bianconi, Esq., the faithful
> Friend of the Immortal Liberator
> And of Ireland, the land of his adoption.

After Catherine's inevitable death in 1854 the Bianconi's returned to Ireland. Within a short time Bianconi had a special Mortuary Chapel built at Boherlahan and the body of Catherine Bianconi was brought home from Italy and interred there.

With all his energy and enthusiasm Bianconi threw himself into the work of improving his estate. All the tenants' houses were slated and wells were sunk in their yards. He bought more land and tried to improve the tillage system. His business still thrived and he spent money generously on worthwhile projects. He became involved in the founding of the Catholic University and bought a house at 86 St. Stephen's Green for that purpose.

The crowning glory of his social aspirations was when he was appointed Deputy Lieutenant of the county in 1863. Already a Justice of the Peace this new position brought him into contact with the highest aristocracy in the land. His landholdings of 9,000 acres put him on a par with the biggest landowners in Tipperary.

Tragedy Strikes the Bianconi Family

The following year, 1864, brought nothing only pain as his only son Charles died in that year. Charles, a spendthrift, had married Eileen FitzSimon, a granddaughter of Daniel O'Connell, by whom he had three daughters. His lavish spending soon led to bankruptcy and Bianconi was reluctant to pay his son's debts. They became estranged and young Charles had to flee to Belgium to escape his creditors. Bianconi was eventually prevailed upon to pay off most of the debts, but the rigours and trauma of his position told on the health of young Charles. He was buried in the family vault at Boherlahan.

His surviving daughter, Mary Ann, fell in love with another O'Connell, Morgan, the nephew of the Liberator. Though much older than Mary Ann, known as Minnie, he was a charming man, and while Bianconi was at first opposed to the marriage, he at last consented and the two were married in the Catholic University Church in Dublin, in 1865. They had one daughter who died young and a son John, who later inherited the Bianconi fortunes.

Bianconi, himself, though in excellent health, fell from a car, when a strap of the harness suddenly snapped, and broke his thigh. He adjusted to life in a wheelchair and lived another ten years, dying in 1875. He was almost ninety years old.

Young John O'Connell was only a boy of four at the time of his grandfather's death. His own father, Morgan, had died suddenly a few months before Bianconi. When he became of age he took the name Bianconi in accordance with the wishes of his grandfather.

He married his cousin, Arabella Burke Hayes and they had only one daughter, Mary Anne, (Molly) who was the co-author of the very fine book *Bianconi King of the Irish Roads*.

Butler of Cahir

Lord Cahir's Siblings Kidnapped

This strange tale is recorded in Dorothea Herbert's book *Reminiscences*. 'Lord Cahir's mother was a poor mendicant woman in the town of Cahir for many years and winnowed corn for her subsistence. When the late Lord Cahir died his expectants found out that this old woman's children were next heirs to his Lordship. They had them kidnapped and secretly conveyed to France where they were reared in miserable poverty. Mrs. Jefferies[4], a sister of the Chancellor, Lord Fitzgibbon, passing through Cahir, heard at an Inn, the history of the old beggar woman and her two children.

She sent for the woman and took notes of her tale, which she laid before the Chancellor. On further investigation the whole was proved to be fact and the Chancellor procured warrants for bringing the children over (to England).

Mrs. Jefferies' daughter was in a convent in France being educated and when Mrs. Jefferies went over to bring her daughter home she undertook the guardianship of the children. They were found in a miserable garret, all overgrown with hair. Mrs. Jefferies had them educated and then made a match for her daughter with the young Lord Cahir[5].

---

[4] Wife of John Jeffreys, Blarney, Co. Cork.
[5] His name was Richard Butler and he was reared as a Protestant.

The Chancellor was much enraged with this proceeding and threatened to imprison his sister and niece for inveigling the young heir but Mrs. Jefferies's cleverness got her over it.

They all came to Ireland and took Dowager Lady Cahir from her winnowing sheet to enjoy her new title and live with her son. They now settled at Cahir.

Lady Cahir was a beautiful little creature, wild with spirits and very affable, but she cursed and swore tremendously. In the metropolis she was chief leader of Fashion and Ton, an uncommonly elegant woman.'

Lord Cahir was restored to his estates by a special Act of Parliament in the reign of Queen Anne. He was confirmed in his estate of 10,000 acres. The restriction on Catholic inheritance was not apparently enforced in his case.

The Origin of the Butlers of Cahir

The Butler association with Cahir began with James Gallda Butler, the illegitimate son of the 3rd. Earl of Ormonde who was born around the year 1400. His mother was Catherine, the daughter of the Earl of Desmond.

James Gallda, of Cahir, was appointed by his brother, the 4th Earl of Ormonde, to be the keeper of the county with the right to maintenance of the necessary troops.[6] This appointment was disastrous as James Gallda had his own agenda and was closely involved with the Desmonds who were rivals of the Ormondes in Munster.

This rivalry ripened into enmity when the War of the Roses broke out in England between the Houses of York and Lancaster. The Ormondes supported the House of Lancaster and the Desmonds that of York. That bitter English war found expression in Ireland when the forces of the Butlers of Ormonde and the Fitzgeralds of Desmond fought a battle at Pilltown in 1462. On that occasion the Ormondes were defeated. This long running dispute continued intermittently until 1565 when the last private battle fought in Ireland took place at Affane, Co. Waterford. The Desmonds were defeated on that day.

---

[6] Eoghan O'Neill *The Golden Vale of Ivowen*

Butler of Cahir

When Piers Rua, whose mother was Sadbh Kavanagh, daughter of the King of Leinster, became the 8th Earl he set about bringing peace between the warring factions. His efforts culminated in what became known as the Composition of Clonmel, a fairly straightforward treaty between the various interests.

As to the Cahir Butlers there were two main items of the agreement that concerned them particularly. The arbiters directed that the Earl should deliver the manor of Cahir with its appurtenances to Edmund Butler, the Baron of Cahir, on condition that Edmund and all his heirs 'shall be in all things faithful to the Earl and his heirs'. The other agreement stated that whenever any stranger should attack Edmund or his country, then all horsemen, Scots, footmen, gentlemen and husbandmen were to rise in defence of Edmund and Mac Ui Phiarais (the ancestor of the Butler Barons of Dunboyne), provided that no regular war would begin or continue without the consent of the Earl.

Another important section deprived the Cahir Butlers of some of their illegal revenues such as coyne and livery and cudihy[7] for his followers. Henceforth they were not allowed to keep their own private army or exact forced labour for the building or repair of their castle or houses.

Edmund was the son of James the first 'Baron'[8] of Cahir. His second son James was soon in breach of the Composition and in 1519 he was arrested and detained by Piers Rua. He seems to have appropriated the goods, profits, rents and tithes of the rectory of Tibroughney. He was released on condition that he restored the goods to the rectory. Eight of the foremost men of the area had to pledge £100 each for his good behaviour.[9] James was later made Sheriff of the county.

A few years later, Thomas Butler, the heir to the manor of Cahir was in dispute himself with Piers Rua and on this occasion had

---

[7] From the Gaelic *cuid oiche* or night suppers.
[8] They were given the title of Baron by the Earl of Ormonde to signify their lordship of the manor of Cahir but later in 1524 they received the official title of Baron from the King.
[9] These were Thomas, Geoffrey and John Prendergast, the Treasurer of Lismore, William, Thomas and David O'Lonergan and John O'Donnell.

to reaffirm the articles of the Composition of Clonmel. It would seem that he had resorted to the coyne and livery and taking of cudihys as well as forced labour and unfair exactions. Thomas's friends, too, had to sign pledges of good behaviour, but this time it was much more severe. They had to sign pledges of £500 each.[10] Thomas Butler was created (officially) 1st Baron of Cahir by the king in 1524.

Cahir Castle (courtesy Irish Architectural Archive)

The Barons of Cahir seemed to continue living in peace until the death of James the 9th Earl of Ormonde in 1546.[11] The new Earl, Thomas (Black Tom), was only a boy of fourteen and the Butlers of Cahir and Dunboyne became restless and ambitious. Their followers committed many robberies and thefts from the Earl's lands during the period.

The Lord Deputy of the time was prevailed upon to try to settle the affairs of the disputing Butlers and in 1549 he appointed

---

[10] In addition to many of those mentioned above others who signed and pledged the £500 were St. John of St. Johnstown, John Comyn of Kilconnell, James Og Wall, James Keating of Moorestown, James Walsh of Rathronan, James Laffin of Greystown and numerous Butlers.

[11] He was poisoned along with his stewart and sixteen of his servants at a supper at Ely House, Holborn.

commissioners to enquire into the affair and recommend any solutions. They found that the Dowager Countess of Ormonde (the mother of Black Tom) had suffered unjustly at the hands of the Cahir Butlers. They ordered that the Baron of Cahir should pay compensation to all those injured and restore any goods that had been stolen or repay their value. Failing that he was ordered to deliver up a number of his followers who included many O'Donnells, Prendergasts, Hogans and Lonergans.

The Butlers of Cahir in the 17th/18th Centuries

Not much is known about the Barons of Cahir until the middle of the 17th century when George Mathew of Thurles married Eleanor Butler, the daughter of Lord Dunboyne and widow of Lord Cahir (another Butler). George raised her young son, the 4th Lord Cahir, and when he was of age married him off to his niece, Elizabeth.

In common with the all the Butlers, including the Earl of Ormonde the Cahir lands were declared forfeit after the Cromwellian wars but were restored in 1662 when Charles II was restored to the monarchy in England.

The Butlers were held in high esteem by the people of Tipperary and during the years following that terrible upheaval poems were still written in praise of the Butlers of Cahir.[12]

Since the Cahirs were Catholic they were lucky to have held on to their lands during the penal times. The 5th Lord Cahir, Theobald Butler, had only one son, Thomas, so the provisions of the penal laws on inheritance did not affect him, as he inherited before 1703. However Thomas, the 6th Lord Cahir, had five sons and in theory the estate should have been divided amongst them.

To avoid this happening sophisticated legal devices were used. The estate was vested in trustees and subsequently mortgaged at various times in the 1750s with the proviso that it would not revert to the owner until the borrowed money was repaid.[13] In effect this meant

---

[12] The fact that the Butlers gave long leases to other pre Cromwellian Anglo Irish and Irish families was a major factor in their popularity.
[13] ibid.

that the person or institution that advanced the money was the legal owner for the time being. Lord Cahir was conveniently absent from the area at this time and his agent was a very competent man, named Martin Murphy from Waterford.

When the 6th Lord died in 1744 he was succeeded by James his eldest son. James now became the 7th Lord. As well as having four brothers, James had two sisters, both of whom died unmarried. One of his brothers died young and another seems to have remained at home and died unmarried also. The Lord Cahir was an absentee landlord[14] who had an income of £10,000 in 1775.

By virtue of the fact that he spent most of his time abroad he escaped the turmoil of the 1760s when the polarized attitude of the Protestant Gentry culminated in the judicial murder of Fr. Sheehy.[15] It is significant though, that one of the co-accused of Fr. Sheehy, James Farrell, who with Edmund Sheehy and James Buxton was hanged in Clogheen in 1766, was a close relative of Lord Cahir.[16] The fact that the head tenants on the Cahir estate were the Catholic Keating, Baldwin and Nagle families made the Protestant gentry nervous. A report on the trials of 1766 remarked of them that 'they were very respectable as they lived in affluence and with reputation, associated with the gentlemen of the neighbourhood with whom they lived in the highest hospitality, frequently receiving and returning visits'.[17] Robert Keating, James Nagle and John Baldwin had been arrested on suspicion of involvement with the Whiteboys and of plotting a French invasion. All three were charged with treason but were acquitted.[18]

There was general distress in 1784 as a result of bad weather conditions leading to the death of cattle. This in turn resulted in ruin, emigration and farms being abandoned or surrendered, as the tenants could not pay the rents. Lord Cahir, to his credit, cancelled arrears, accepted surrenders and abated former rents. The bad weather of 1784 was only a hiccup as the level of income on the Cahir estate grew from

---

[14] He came to live for a period at Cahir Castle in the mid 1770s. - T. Power in *Land, Politics and Society in 18th century Tipperary*.
[15] For a full account of the Fr. Sheehy case see Bagwell in this volume.
[16] Eoghan O'Neill in *The Golden Vale of Ivowen*
[17] *Gentlemen's and London Magazine*
[18] T. Power in *Land, Politics and Society in 18th century Tipperary*.

£10,000 in 1775 to £36,000 in 1809. The Butler owners also benefited from the rents of Cahir town.[19]

As with many Catholic gentry families younger sons often went abroad and entered the French (military) service. So it was with Pierce Butler and Thomas[20], brothers of the 7th Lord Cahir.

James was unmarried and when he died in 1786 the estate passed to his brother Pierce. Since the penal laws on inheritance had been repealed in 1778 there was now no difficulty in the succession.

The Act of 1778, which gave an enormous measure of relief to the Catholics, was widely welcomed by the Catholics in Tipperary. The main features of the Act were (1) the removal of the requirement that Catholic property had to be divided among the surviving sons. (2) Leases could now be given for more than 31 years. (3) The removal of the decree that a son who converted would get immediate possession making his parent a tenant for life only. The Act would only apply to people who took the oath of allegiance. In Tipperary county over 900 people took the oath. This number probably represented the vast majority of Catholic landowners in the county and included Archbishop Butler and many of his clergy.

As a result of the passage of the Act two tenants of Lord Cahir, James Nagle of Garnvella and Robert Keating of Knockagh had their interest in leases confirmed.[21]

With the re-emergence of considerable agrarian unrest, the American war of Independence and threatened French invasions Volunteer Corps were founded all over Ireland. The corps on the Cahir estate was composed of Catholics and was commanded by Pierce Butler, Lord Cahir's brother. Each corps was comprised of about forty rank and file members drawn from the head tenantry or from friends or associates of the colonel.

When James Butler died he was succeeded by Pierce Butler, who only survived his brother two years and died in 1788. The estate then passed to James Butler of Glengall, the 9th Lord, a cousin of

---

[19] ibid
[20] Thomas was sent to France to enter military service at the age of 16, in 1737. The following year he was made second Lieutenant in Dillon's regiment and was later promoted to Captain in Lally's regiment. He fought at the Battle of Fontenoy. – Ibid.
[21] T. Power in *Land Politics and Society in 18th century Tipperary*

Pierce. James died in the same year as Pierce (1788)[22]. His son Richard became the 10th Lord Cahir and 1st Earl of Glengall and we have recounted his story at the beginning.[23] He was twenty-five years old at the time of his succession.

The Cahir estate did not go unnoticed in the period of unrest when the Whiteboys were active. In 1800, Alexander Mollison, Lord Cahir's steward, was murdered. It would appear from some local evidence that the instigators of the rural unrest in the area were the tenants on the Cahir estate. This situation may have arisen because prior to 1800 the estate agent,[24] who had granted long leases, was replaced by Scott, an attorney and later by Mollison.

Richard the 10th Lord Cahir

Richard the restored heir made an unsuccessful attempt, in the early 1800s to reduce the period of the leases on his lands, where the middlemen held leases of 61 years. The middlemen in turn sublet extensively so that the estate was divided into an array of small sub tenancies from which the middlemen reaped large profit rents. One of the later Lord Cahirs, possibly Richard, said that 'the estate was loaded with paupers' and the leases were 'shamefully abused with the lands being sub-let and ruined and the farmers pauperized by the leasees'.[25] The Cahir estate leases did not change until the 1840s when the long leases expired.

Lord Cahir carried out extensive improvements to his estate where he embellished two miles of a demesne on either side of the Suir. A visitor later remarked that 'finely planted and well stocked with deer the scenery was bold and romantic and the river a fine deep stream gliding through a rich and fertile land'. He had his own band,

---

[22] He had two brothers in the church who may have been responsible for the abduction of the young Richard Butler.
[23] His mother Dame Sarah Baroness Cahir converted to Protestantism in 1789 – *Inch Papers*
[24] This may have been Martin Murphy, the merchant from Waterford.
[25] T. Power Land, *Politics & Society in 18th century Tipperary*.

which played in the town square of Cahir and was known as Lord Cahir's band.[26]

Law & Order on the Butler Estates

Just as the appointment of more professional agents in the 1780s can be viewed as a reassertion of the landlord's power, so also can the revival of manor courts in that decade. These institutions were largely medieval in origin though some came into existence in the seventeenth century. About 1650 there were thirty-seven locations, which had manorial jurisdiction, but by the 1830s this number had fallen to six.

Functionally the manor court was divided into a court leet and a court baron. In the former, which was convened twice yearly by the manor's seneschal, who was appointed by the landowner, matters like land boundaries, roads, regulation of markets, weights and measures were dealt with. The court baron, also summoned by the seneschal, adjudicated in cases concerning the recovery of cash debts (£5 or under), promissory notes (£10 or under), and trespass. The court proceedings for the manor of Coolkill near Thurles in 1790 show it to have been mainly taken up with disputes between tenants, adjudicating small debts, and awarding costs.

Lord Cahir appointed a seneschal for his three manors in 1802, as did Lord Llandaff for his manor of Thurles in 1817. The revival of these courts reflected the desire of certain landlords to reassert control over their estates, which in Lord Cahir's case had been sharply diminished in the 1780s.[27]

Richard Butler stood for election in 1818 and topped the poll ahead of the Mathew candidate with Prittie coming a close third. He resigned the seat however, in the following year, as he had been elevated to the peerage as the 1st Earl Glengall. He was opposed to the plan to divide Tipperary on the grounds that the cost would be exorbitant. He had survived a duel in 1826 arising from his being

---

[26] M.O'Connell Bianconi and S.J. Watson in *Bianconi King of the Irish Roads*
[27] This loss of control was evidenced by a rise in lawlessness. Lord Cahir's stewart was murdered in 1799. – *Finn's Leinster Journal*

allegedly libeled in *Age* magazine.[28] He supported Catholic Emancipation and in 1828 he had given a free site and a substantial sum of money towards the erection of a Catholic chapel at Dunhill. This was at odds with his attending a 'Protestant' dinner in Morrison's Hotel in honour of the Earl of Winchelsea in the course of which 'he confessed his error' in voting for Emancipation.

Richard and his wife were very prominent at all the social functions in the county and as we have seen his wife, apart from being elegant was lively and extrovert. They were the leading figures at the Cahir Ball in the Assembly Rooms. Richard was the President of the Tipperary Agriculture Society and was chairman of many of the local bodies.

Richard Butler the Last Lord Cahir

Richard had one son Richard and on the death of the 10th Lord Cahir and 1st Earl of Glengall, he became the 11th Lord and 2nd Earl. He married Margaret Mellish of Essex in 1834, in London. After a prolonged honeymoon abroad they arrived back in Cahir where they were met by the usual cheering crowd of tenants, who unharnessed the horses and pulled the carriage themselves. These scenes of jubilation were accompanied by the firing of cannon.

The new Earl spent much of his time abroad. He had a yacht built, a craft of some 500 tons, which was launched at Cowes the following year. He named it *The Margaret* in deference to his wife.

A combination of bad luck, the Famine, foreign holidays, the town house (now Cahir House Hotel), a marine residence in the Isle of Wight, a London house at 34 Grosvenor Square, the building of St. Paul's Church of Ireland and an Erasmus Smith school in Cahir debilitated his finances. He went bankrupt in 1855 and the estate had to be sold. John Sadleir, the unfortunate banker from Tipperary,

---

[28] D. Murphy *The Two Tipperarys*

bought the estate for £68,000.²⁹ The Earl's daughter Margaret and her husband Richard Charteris re-purchased the estates later.³⁰

The Swiss Cottage, early 1800s (Courtesy Dept of the Environment)

John Sadleir, the unfortunate banker from Tipperary, bought the estate for £68,000. The Earl's daughter Margaret and her husband Richard Charteris re-purchased the estates later.³¹

The last Earl who died in 1858 and his countess who died in 1864, were buried in the grounds of St. Paul's Church, Cahir, together with a daughter and his mother.

Lady Margaret erected a fountain in Cahir in 1876. The purpose of the fountain was to supply water to the town centre. It was piped from the Galtee Mountains. The fountain was erected as a memorial to her husband the Hon. Richard Charteris.

Lt.- Col. Hon. Richard Charteris was the son of the 9th Earl of Weymss from Scotland. He died in 1874 aged 51. Lady Margaret and Richard had four children – Elinor (d.1940), Maud Emily (d. 1945),

---

[29] When the Joint Stock Bank of Tipperary crashed in 1856 he committed suicide. At the time of his death he had an overdraft of £250,000.
[30] D. Murphy *The Two Tipperarys*
[31] D. Murphy *The Two Tipperarys*

Lt.-Col. Richard Butler (d. 1961) and Captain Edmund (d.1939). Elinor and Maud Emily were both married and Maud Emily is represented today by the Wynne-Finch family from Gwynedd, Wales. Elinor's descendants include the Burnett family of London. Neither of the sons had any children. Lt.-Col. Richard lived in Cahir Castle until his death in 1961.

Between 1876 and the end of the century the Charteris Estate was responsible for the building of the town reservoir. Water was then supplied on tap to the houses of the town for an annual charge. The local council paid the Charteris estate for the water up to the early 1960s when the estate was finally sold.

Index

Baldwin, 6, 23
Ball, 11, 27
Belgium, 17
Beresford, 8, 9
Bessborough, 15
Bianconi, 1, 2, 4, 5, 6, 7, 8, 9,
   10, 11, 12, 13, 14, 15, 16, 17,
   26
Black, 21, 22
Boherlahan, 16, 17
Burke, 17
Butler, 18, 19, 20, 22, 24, 25,
   26
   Black Tom, 21
   Edmund, 20
   Elenor, widow of Lord
      Cahir, 22
   Pierce, 8th Lord Cahir, 24
   Piers Rua, 20
Buxton, 23
Cahir, 6, 8, 18, 19, 20, 21, 22,
   23, 24, 25, 26, 27, 28
Carrick, 6
Cashel, 8, 14, 15
Charles II, 13, 22
Charteris, 28
Clogheen, 23
Clonmel, 5, 6, 7, 8, 9, 12, 13,
   20, 21
Coolkill, 26
Coopers, 15
Cork, 18
Cowes, 27
Del Vecchio, 7

Dillon, 24
Dublin, 5, 7, 9, 17
Dunboyne, 20, 21, 22
Dundrum, 15
Dunhill, 26
England, 18, 19, 22
Faroni, 5, 6
Farrell, 23
Fitzgibbon, 18
FitzSimon, 16
France, 18, 24
Glengall
   Earl of, 24, 25, 26, 27
Golden, 19, 23
Hayes, 7, 9, 17
Hearn, 4, 12
Herbert, 18
Hogans, 22
Inch, 25
Isle of Wight, 28
Italy, 5, 11, 15, 16
Jefferies, 18, 19
Keating, 21, 23, 24
Knockagh, 24
Lalor, 11
Limerick, 6, 8
Lismore, 20
Llandaff, 26
London, 5, 6, 10, 12, 23, 27, 28
Lonergans, 22
Long
   Captain, 14
Longfield, 14
Marlfield, 7

Index

Mathew, 6, 15, 22, 26
   Fr. Theobald, 6
Mellish, 27
Minehan, 4
Mollison, 25
Morgan, 17
Morrison, 27
Munster, 5, 19
Murphy, 23, 25, 26, 28
Murray
   Archbishop, 9
Nagle, 23, 24
Napoleon, 6
O'Connell, 7, 9, 10, 11, 12, 13, 15, 16, 17, 26
O'Donnells, 22
O'Neill, 19, 23
Ormonde, 19, 20, 21, 22
Passage, 6
Peel, 10
Petty, 13
Power, 23, 24, 25
Prendergast, 20
Prendergasts, 22
Prittie, 26

Queen Anne, 19
Rathronan, 21
Ribaldi, 6
Rice, 6
Rome, 15, 16
Sadleir
   John, 28
Scott, 25
Sheehy, 23
Smith, 28
Thurles, 4, 6, 8, 22, 26
Tipperary, 1, 2, 5, 11, 16, 22, 23, 24, 25, 26, 27, 28
Villiers Stuart, 9, 10
Wall, 21
Walsh, 21
Waterford, 5, 6, 8, 19, 23, 25
Watson, 26
Westminster, 13
Whiteboys, 23, 25
Winchelsea
   Earl of, 27
Wyse, 11

Printed in Great Britain
by Amazon.co.uk, Ltd.,
Marston Gate.